LEVEL
1

Trains

Amy Shields

NATIONAL
GEOGRAPHIC
Washington, D.C.

To the Silver Star, Empire, Vermonter, and
Adirondack trains, long may they run.

All photos of Gary the Engineer by Becky Hale/ NationalGeographicStock.com

Library of Congress Cataloging-in-Publication Data

Shields, Amy.
Trains / by Amy Shields.
p. cm.—(National geographic readers)
ISBN 978-1-4263-0777-5 (pbk. : alk. paper)—ISBN 978-1-4263-0778-2 (library binding : alk. paper)
1. Railroads—United States—History—Juvenile literature. 2. Railroad travel—United States—History—Juvenile literature.
I. Title.
TF23.S54 2011
625.1—dc22

2010050659

cover, All Canada Photos/ Alamy; 1, Steve Crise/ Transtock/ Corbis; 2, iStockphoto; 4 (top left), Jean Brooks/ Robert Harding World Imagery/ Corbis;
4 (top right), Steve Eshom; 4 (bottom left), Arvind Garg/ Corbis; 4 (bottom right), Scott Barrow/ Corbis; 5 (top left), Benjamin Rondel/ Corbis;
5 (top right), Photolibrary/ Corbis; 5 (bottom), Kevin Fleming/ Corbis; 6-7, Glow Images/ Getty Images; 8-9, Nigel Hicks/ Dorling Kindersley/ Getty
Images; 9 (inset), Larry Dale Gordon/ Photographer's Choice/ Getty Images; 10 (top), Richard T. Nowitz/ Corbis; 11 (top), altrendo travel/ Stockbyte/
Getty Images; 11 (bottom), Chris Harris/ All Canada Photos/ Corbis; 12, Bettmann/ Corbis; 13 (Background), Design Pics Images/ Fotosearch;
13 (inset), Corbis; 15 (top), H. Armstrong Roberts/ Retrofile/ Getty Images; 15 (bottom), Bettmann/ Corbis; 16 (top), Lee Prince/ Shutterstock;
16 (center), Nathan G./epa/Corbis; 16 (bottom), Justin Horrocks/ iStockphoto.com; 17 (top), Martin Ruetschi/ Keystone/Corbis; 17 (center), Diana
Walters/ iStockphoto.com; 17 (bottom), National Postal Museum/ Smithsonian Institution; 18-19, Kent Kobersteen/ NationalGeographicStock.com;
19 (inset), James Lauritz/ Digital Vision/ Getty Images; 20, H. Lefebvre/ClassicStock/Corbis; 21 (top), H. Armstrong Roberts/ Classicstock;
21 (bottom), Bettmann/ Corbis; 22 (Background), Design Pics Images/ Fotosearch; 23, courtesy Royale Indian Rail Tours Ltd.; 24-25, Greg Dale/
NationalGeographicStock.com; 26-27, Bryan F. Peterson/ Corbis; 29, Paul Miller/ Bloomberg via Getty Images; 30, Kazumasa Yanai/ Getty Images;
31, mountainberryphoto/ iStockphoto.com; 32 (top right), H. Armstrong Roberts/ Retrofile/ Getty Images; 32 (bottom left), Bryan F. Peterson/
Corbis; 32 (bottom right), Kent Kobersteen/ NationalGeographicStock.com;

National Geographic supports K–12 educators with ELA Common Core Resources.
Visit natgeoed.org/commoncore for more information.

Printed in the United States of America
Paperback: 15/WOR/7

Table of Contents

Lots of Trains

Steam train, freight train,
circus train, cold train.

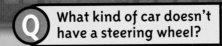

Grain train, coal train,
people-on-the-go train.

All Aboard!

Have you been on a steam train ride? Did you hear the wheels **clackety-clack** on the track? Did you hear the **WOOOO-woo** whistle? Did the **ding-ding-ding** bell ring at the train crossing?

I'm Gary and this is my train. I am the engineer.

Train Talk

ENGINEER: A person who drives the train

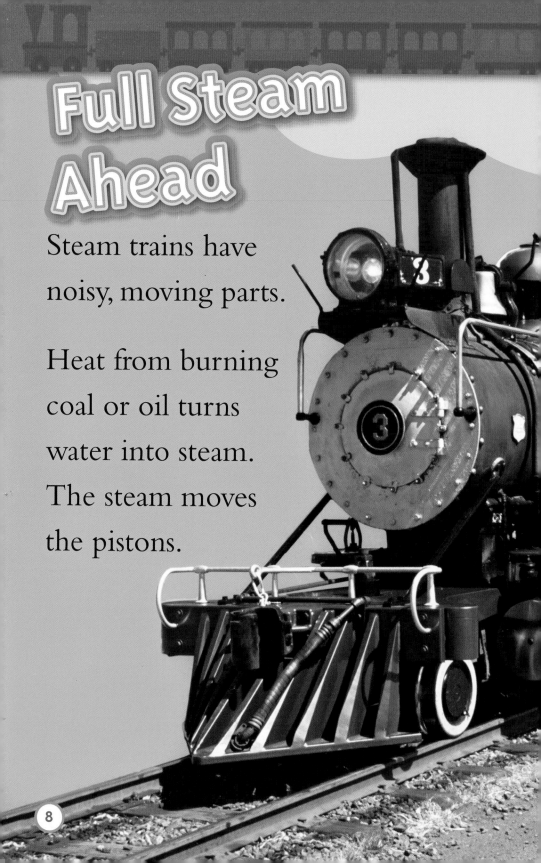

Full Steam Ahead

Steam trains have noisy, moving parts.

Heat from burning coal or oil turns water into steam. The steam moves the pistons.

The pistons move the rods. The rods turn the wheels and move the train on the tracks.

rod

Trains have special wheels that roll on tracks. Most train tracks are made of steel rails and wood ties. The rails are nailed to the ties.

steel rails

wood ties

Cars cannot drive on train rails.

Trains follow tracks over valleys.

They roll on tracks through mountains.

4612 4612

A New America

About 150 years ago, Chinese and Irish people helped build the train tracks. They became new Americans.

When the tracks were done, they stretched across America. More people moved west. Towns were built along the rail tracks. Banks and stores were built. Trains brought them money and gold.

Many trains got held up by robbers.

Robbers wanted to steal the money and gold. Butch Cassidy and the Sundance Kid were robbers. They robbed trains with their gang. Then they rode off on their horses. They split the loot at their hideout, the Hole-in-the-Wall.

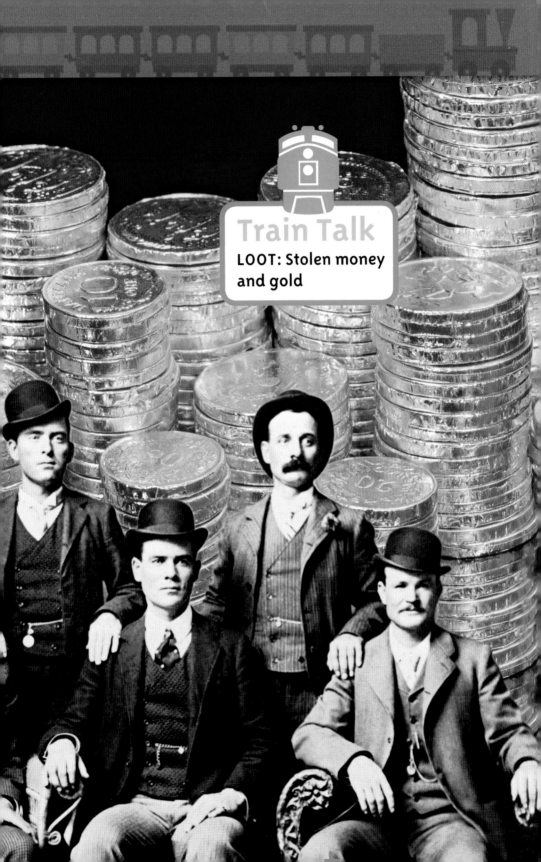

LOOT: Stolen money and gold

Cool Things About Trains

1

Some bullet trains float magnetically above the rails.

2

The Fairy Queen in India is one of the oldest running steam trains.

3

People who love trains are called railfans. They take vacations to go trainspotting.

4 The longest train tunnel in the world is 35 miles long. It goes through the Alps mountains. It will open in 2017.

5 Many train stations are called Union Station. These are stations used by different train lines.

6 A puppy was found on a mail car in 1888. The mailmen named him Owney. He rode the mail trains and became their lucky charm.

Train Tricks

What happens when trains reach the end of the track? Tracks in a rail yard lead to a turntable. The locomotive rolls onto the turntable.

Whirrrrr. The turntable turns. The locomotive rolls off in a new direction.

Train Talk

TURNTABLE:
A piece of train track that can be turned

A turntable is a cool train invention.
Here are more cool inventions.
People thought of ways to ride
train tracks even
without trains.

Look at some of these inventions.

mule-drawn train car

handcar

Passenger Trains

Now there are train tracks all over the world.

People take trains to get to work. They take train ride vacations, too.

The Maharajas' Express is a train in India. It is called a palace on wheels.

Say *ma-ha-RAH-jas*

It was built for royalty. People take vacations on this train. It is a nice, slow ride through the country.

Want a faster ride? Bullet trains
are fast like bullets. These trains
go more than 275 miles an hour.
Bullet trains run on train tracks.

Some bullet trains are pulled by
locomotives. Some have motors for
each car. Bullet trains are passenger
trains, for people.

Bullet trains are electric. They have pantographs on top of some of the cars. Wires overhead pass electricity to the pantographs.

pantograph

Train Talk

PANTOGRAPH: Metal arms on a train's roof that catch electricity from wires above

Say *PAN-toe-graf*

Electricity comes from coal, the same coal that powers steam engines.

Freight Trains

Freight trains carry stuff, like sneakers and cell phones. The longest freight trains are two miles long. These trains have diesel locomotives. The locomotives in front pull. The locomotives in back push.

Most of the stuff in your house rode on a train at one time.

Say *DEE-zul*

diesel locomotive

When trains roll past, railmen stand aside and watch. Next time a train passes you, wave hi to the mighty train rolling **clackety-clack** down the track.